DIVINING
THE LANDSCAPE

DIVINING
THE LANDSCAPE

POEMS BY

Diane Jarvenpa

Minnesota Voices Project Number 74

New Rivers Press 1996

Copyright © 1996 by Diane Jarvenpa
Library of Congress Catalog Card Number 96-067-819
ISBN 0-89823-168-x
All Rights Reserved
Edited by Vivian Vie Balfour
Editorial Assistance by Carol Rutz
Book design by Ronna Hammer
Typesetting by Peregrine Graphics Services
Cover illustration by Lelde Kalmite

New Rivers Press is a non-profit literary press dedicated to publishing the very best emerging writers in our region, nation, and world.

The publication of *Divining the Landscape* has been made possible by generous grants from the Jerome Foundation, the Metropolitan Regional Arts Council (from an appropriation by the Minnesota Legislature), the National Endowment for the Arts, the North Dakota Council on the Arts, the South Dakota Arts Council, Target Stores, Dayton's and Mervyn's by the Dayton Hudson Foundation, and the James R. Thorpe Foundation.

Additional support has been provided by the Elmer L. and Eleanor J. Andersen Foundation, the Beim Foundation, Bush Foundation, General Mills Foundation, Liberty State Bank, the McKnight Foundation, the Minnesota State Arts Board (through an appropriation by the Minnesota Legislature), the Star Tribune/Cowles Media Company, the Tennant Company Foundation, and the contributing members of New Rivers Press. New Rivers is a member agency of United Arts.

Divining the Landscape has been manufactured in Canada for New Rivers Press, 420 North 5th Street, Suite 910, Minneapolis, MN 55401. First Edition.

For Donald Brundage
and for my mother, Aili Jarvenpa

Acknowledgements

The following poems have appeared, some in earlier versions, in these publications:

"Prairie Dreaming Sea" in *Exit 13*; "The Kantele Players" and "Juhannus-Midsummer" in *The Finnish American Reporter*; "Spotted Leopard" and "Apple" in *Loonfeather;* "Polka" in *Mixed Voices: Contemporary Poems About Music,* Milkweed Editions; "Beginnings Of Speech," "Winter Sun," "After The Concert" and "Somewhere Somebody Is Drinking Brandy" in *Sampo: The Magic Mill A collection of Finnish-American writing,* New Rivers Press; "Aubade" in *Poet's On.*

Contents

I

Beginnings of Speech 3
Driving Down Florida 4
Annuals 5
First Fish 6
Muskrats 8
Concert by Segovia 9
The Other Language 10
Forest Creatures 12
Apple 13
The Kantele Players 14
Juhannus–Midsummer 15

II

Prairie Dreaming Sea 19
Winter Sun 20
Never Quite Right 21
Spotted Leopard 23
Bison bison 24
The Succession of the Oak 25
Wild Flowers 26
Before This 27
Töölon Hospital 28
Grandfather 29
My Grandmothers in America 31
Flying Geese 32
For Those of Us Left Behind 33
The Rubble Women 34
Somewhere Someone Is Drinking Brandy 35
Down to the River 36
Polka 38

III

Aubade   41
Bee Song   42
Wedding   43
Poem about Us from Samarkand   44
Uspenski Cathedral   46
Bathtub on Rue Tolosane   47
The Accordion Repairman   48
Sudden Wealth   49
Past Time   50
La'a Kea Farm   51
Orchidaceae   52
Vernal Equinox   53
Summer Comes   54
Things We Think We Cannot See   55
Divining The Landscape   58
After The Concert   59

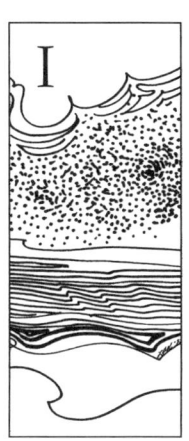

Beginnings of Speech

You sling your voice
over the edge of the crib.
It trembles like a fish
falling to the watery floor
with the penguin and plastic rings.
Your hands, curved pink shrimp,
reach for the stain of sleep,
rubbing the dust from your eyes,
dreams of rabbits running at the moon.
You swim through grass,
wade through kelp beds
as the curtains undulate
across silent windows,
soft green waves.
The warmth of salty baked bread
rises in the dim light
with your voice,
vowels long and deep.
You pitch them like pennies
waiting to hear the echo,
the long arms of morning,
as you stamp at the rim of your canyon.

Driving Down Florida

Stuckey's peanut brittle chipping our teeth,
Elvis ringing in the car like a fever,
our '63 Rambler wagon sliced down the highway.
Passing through the high tide of summer heat,
our young arms hung out the windows,
preparing for towers of splashing palms,
air that spoke of mangoes, dolphin water.
We could already see the shore,
feel the salt seltzer waves
on our bodies pale as milkweed.
Dusk bloomed as tiny towns streamed by us
fast as the trunks of chinaberry,
small houses lighting one by one.
We lay back in our seats
sleepy white moths caught in a moving jar
as the baseball game sent out its slow hum
of fielder's choice and double play.
In the dark we came to understand
that feeling of surrender
as the perfume of orange trees
gathered in our half-sleep;
the magic of my father's foot
coaxing miles under the engine
and my mother's voice calling out
each junction off the map like poems
from an odd ancient scroll.

Annuals

In the blaze of the backyard
my mother bent at her task,
silently cupping out the black dirt,
firmly inserting the loamy squares,
green stems squirting out their middle.
She ignored the noisy hollyhocks of her neighbors,
attaching herself to her heliotrope and verbena
liking the way they took hold of her yard
instead of only climbing out for sky.
There had to be lots of annuals,
leaving for good in the fall
so come spring the flower bed lay bare as death,
an old ruin wiped by hard wind
until my mother worked her hands.
And in time the sticky green stems
budded and flowered in purples and rose
like the brushstrokes on the French canvas
we had seen hanging in the art museum.
The long curve of my mother's flower bed
stretched the length of the suburban yard,
a piece of elegance balanced
between swing set and clothesline,
as if to say, here,
this is different,
yes, this is how it can be.

First Fish

in memory of my father

Water lapped blue tongues
against the boat
as you baited the hooks in silence.
Casting out we waited for bobbers
to disappear, driven below by trout or pike.
Under the sun's arrow
I laid back, a lazy target,
pale starfish in my life jacket
when it caught.
My arms felt its long arcing pattern
until the glittering skin came up
in the seltzer of its slashing tail.
A young ugly rock bass
caught noiseless in the spiral
prison of raw air
twisted on the hook.
You took it from me
and when it beat against
the bottom of the boat
I didn't mind for it was mine.
Like passing the rites of any religion
I had finally entered the songline
of my family, family of fishermen,
and I held it proudly
as you took my picture.
But knowing it was too soon,
that many small offerings
still stood off before me,
you made me give it back;
like a promise you made
each time you entered the water
with a child, binding yourself
to small beauties that break
in the silence of the earth.
Eyes still glistening
it slipped under and away from me

thankful as a parachutist,
leaving the tracks of its beating body
in my small hands
that found themselves filling up
with unknown choices
in cool blue water.

Muskrats

As soon as birds arced
their skywriting in the fall,
the garage would begin to fill up.
If a careless hand slipped
and hit a gland, the smell surged
like blood, trembling long in the air,
taking your lungs.
All the stretchers
crossing their cold wire,
pushing at fur,
hung throughout the room
like scuffed bells
ringing their inaudible whispers,
sure places to get the tender shoots,
what grasses held up warmth at night.
The idleness of my childhood
drew me to them,
the garage almost dark.
They hung, slippered like
pieces of cloud made solid,
half-sleeves of wildness
far from pink bedrooms.
And my mother would always say,
"Don't go down there now."
And I would just keep going
as quietly as they move
in the folds of the marsh,
as quietly as my brothers,
like any boys, laid their traps
with multitudes of wonder
at their own hands.
When everyone had left the room,
I would visit them,
slick membranes peeled off bone,
pulled like taffy, dried like sea kelp.
They floated over me,
telling me how the earth was constantly
changing its colors,
telling me in the single bead of blood
at the bottom of the washtub
how things roar in total silence.

Concert by Segovia

From Sor to De Visée to Albeniz,
from bird, mountain, rainstorm.
Lemon trees and bitter almond
filled the auditorium,
the dental hygienist in the third row
wore giant tortoise shell combs
and held a painted lace fan.
A musical vendor, his fat muscled fingers
threw sound out to every seat:
a peanut bag of Poulenc,
a foil encrusted Bach prelude
to feed the many hungry.
That night before I went to bed,
I took my guitar from its case
and laid it on the empty twin bed
reserved for guests,
its perfect curve
shining in the moonlight,
odd partner to the scars of my adolescence.
And I put it at the foot of my own bed
before I fell asleep,
no longer afraid to touch it,
no longer afraid of its many answers.

The Other Language

The grown-ups line their bodies
on the hot upper bench of the sauna,
we children climb the bottom bench
sit inside the thick membrane of heat.
Water hits the rocks
and we bow our heads,
receive the veil of steam.
Clouds take over the room in shapes
of ungodly heat and language.
Mary's father begins a long joke
all the words lost on us kids
except for the punch line
paska housu—"shit pants."
Smiles spread before another blast of steam.

John's mother leans over to scrub his ears,
Finnish syllables spill from her mouth,
pebbles of nonsense through our minds as she
tells some piece of gossip to my mother.
As the room gets hotter
and the dialect further from our ken,
we descend the small knowledge of our bodies,
hearts banging against ribs,
blood rocking in our skulls,
forced beyond our natural breath
and lost inside our parents' other tongue.

All thoughts gone,
we run to the dock and jump,
the lake giving its great slap of cold.
In water we break our silence,
tattoo the air with sounds we understand,
loud dog paddle races
and belly flop competitions.
The adults, hair wet smooth,
sit on lawn chairs on the dock,
tip beer bottles in a circle
ready for the last of the sun.

Again their world returns
with the sounds of their music,
a language that is part of us
but one we will never be a part of;
the hard pain of their non-American childhood past,
entering kindergarten with no English words,
lonely bachelor uncles drinking
and shooting themselves in the barn,
the talk amongst the other town's folk
of Finns and their drunken knife fights
living in tiny backyard shacks,
the stigma assigned to being
wobblies or communists,
all making us a mute third generation.

That distant place our grandparents
stubbornly carried inside them in steerage
passes from their children's hands to ours.
The path is set for us,
but our eyes blink unsure
in the coming and present darkness.

Forest Creatures

I wanted to walk with you in the woods,
watch your faces, egg white in all the greenery,
watch you move quietly
as fish slip through rivers.
While I sat at home with dolls,
your fingers darted, large thick needles
precisely knotting the fishing line,
slitting and gutting the pale pike,
all so easy, clean.
I wanted to walk with you in the forest
as you dropped clouds of smoke and bones
like coins along your trails,
be with you as you drifted into silence,
or running suddenly, two dogs
following an invisible stick.
Out in the after-dinner dark
we would have passed the stars around
as a pan of jewels, seeing marble
in the horns of Taurus, a half-naked woman
in the spilling seeds of the Pleiades.
But I am the odd bottle you found
by the stream bed,
out of place in your surroundings.
You had no fear,
seasons passed through your bodies
in the icy shimmer of the traps you laid,
wreaths of steel pearls in the snow.
And in the summer you went miles away again,
soft plumage of the woods hanging at each portage,
crystalline waters spilling chords of songs,
a sentence something extra in the mouth.
Our parents turned in their bed,
visions of you tossed against the rocks,
but I slept soundly walking pine trails
in the velvet stillness of night.
I alone heard your voices as clear as gunshot
over the tops of trees,
watching the stars,
waiting for me.

Apple

Holding your head
in the palm of my hand,
rolling you out between my fingers,
peeling back the red shell
with my eye teeth, your broken flesh
lies moist and waiting,
a poor boy's champagne.
You course through my body
filling the hollowness
the way dreams answer emptiness
with temporary color.
You roll on
touching old memories,
the many times you gave
yourself up for the child:
how my parents cut away your skin
in jeweled ringlets, presenting me
with the real moon-white slivers.
I took you as a gift from them,
something that was just that moment,
but also something beyond childhood:
a secret confidence
in all the things
I didn't know then
would eventually come to me,
as you did,
the feeling that I would
somehow always remember this.

The Kantele Players

for my teachers
Toivo Alaspää and Martti Pokela

It was as if when they were born,
pulled from their mothers
tiny and red,
their tight fists already held answers
in the arctic light,
seeds of testimony to fight the ghosts.
Somewhere hinged in their fingers
was to be a chronicle
of the inner body dancing.
As children they glided into forests
with the magpies,
listening to the long work of leaves,
wind beating out its information,
the music the water slips into reeds.

Lifting boards to their knees
they measure, cut and build their homes.
The door leads out past long silver strings,
long leashes of sun where woodpeckers and hawks
tip and wing along paperbark birch,
plucking at fruit and singing rock.
Listening to their playing
you feel your own bones lift up
with the knowledge that pure speech
doesn't always touch the tongue,
that light always somehow finds the body.

It was as if they knew
somewhere hinged in their fingers
was a chronicle of the inner body dancing,
of the pure white of flowers unfolding
        in the wood,
       of stone and sea,
       and dream song.

The kantele is a traditional stringed instrument of Finland. It belongs to the family of Baltic psalteries. A harp-like instrument, it is played on a table or on the lap and ranges in size from five to thirty-six strings. Its mythological origins are found in the Kalevela, *the national epic of Finland.*

Juhannus-Midsummer

It begins in the voices of running children
fanning out a summer night and the wide sea
of light finally squeezed out at the horizon.
The cool cloth of wind, folded smooth,
wipes hot foreheads, luminous as snowdrops
as the hidden nest of poison ivy
just waits for that human touch.
From lava to peat bog, beautiful heads
of bonfires ignite evening.
The cottonwoods burst and jingle
and the old lilacs dry up and blow away
into the giant porthole of the season,
the one that calls forth wild leek and blackberries,
the one that calls forth the small child alone
in the deep hull of the unconscious.

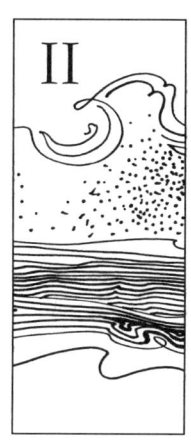

Prairie Dreaming Sea

Prairie gleams in winter
heaving like a permanent cloud,
pitches in driest summer,
listening to its own pale skin
break apart an empty birth.
On this land we are locked
to the slow perfume of soybeans
and scratchy trench music of cornhusks.
As we sleep,
the yawn of Pacific waves
pulls us in our dreams.
We marvel at the long blue mystery of that sea,
the raw spray printing us like desert rock,
the shoreline carving itself
not with rows of ripe wheat
but larch and palm that pass voices
of salt green from throat to long throat.
Some things can't be found
in the soft sheet of ground that spreads
around us, flat like tissue paper.
We turn in our beds, thirsty
for a land that does come to an end,
for bits of conch and beach pea,
jets of salt air blowing crepe
across the skin and deep ocean water
swallowing that hard lump of puritan worry.
As we waken, we feel
the last pitch of a wave inside us,
its dark tide slowly lifting away
past the frozen creek bed,
beyond the work waiting inside the barn.

Winter Sun

The small winter sun
in this northern country
shines like a slice of amber.
I want to hold it in my hands
as it cracks its shell on the sea's wet stone,
and pick out bright threads
to keep in a drawer for some day
that hangs like a wet sheet.
But it isn't mine to hold.
I still don't know enough of
its equatorial flame salting
the back of my neck,
or the distant flashlight beam of
Antarctica barely reaching my shoulders.
It can fool me as I hunger
to shake winter's death hold.
It draws me to the window
like a bather to a beach.
I want to learn
yet I can't give in to
the power in its lost music
behind a drape of cloud,
soaking a day black.
I'm unable to follow the pointed arrow of birds,
ripping through the winds
led on by its constant robe of yellow ash.
So I wait for the slow summer descent
over the bay,
watching its seasonal flux
like a map of Venetian waterways
that you experience,
but never come to understand;
to someday know its flame
not as a distant thing,
or an endurance;
not the breathing out over and over
of an endless star,
but also a breathing in.

Never Quite Right

What can I do with this night,
one more winter night with its glassy surface?
Ideas caught outside on icy branches
hang out of reach like songs of tuneless birds.
For a moment I believe in the cold,
the way the moon glows a pure lily
lighting the frozen windows of my room.
Then it rises and fades so small and cool,
a slender reed of white pressed into the sky,
everything too quiet.

I don't remember my own thoughts in winter
just the empty breath of desire.
So I sleep it off,
wake up again like the weather.
In August when heat rises
from cracks in the blacktop
and the sun rolls down my skin
witness to a body limp as a weed,
I think—January.
The word grows on my tongue
a myriad of tiny icicles,
air hard as iron and long white hills
of snow that dump and swirl
like liquid caught fast, sweet cream.

And in January when wind chills slam
the back of my head and the car engine
does a final pirouette under a tiny
candle flame of sun,
I think—August.
Spicy greens of deep grass,
catalpas and grape ivy.
The rich, thick language of peach melbas
at midnight, air heavy with lake water swale
and the pollen of hydrangea and tea roses
bending to the lip of stifling heat.
They go on,
early frosts and long heat waves

pinning themselves to my doubting flesh,
thin dresses of apricot and silver.
And I always crawl under their shadows
trying to learn the sound
they make in the earth.
To get it straight one time,
cold and hot,
and never quite right.

Spotted Leopard

You fix your tired gaze over our heads
as though peeling back the room
exposing the stubble earth and wind
alive with hornbills and acacias;
our children bore you
and you think you miss the smell
of balsam flowers.
Here there is only an occasional orchid
the gardener coaxes from phony rock
and the acrid scent of disinfectant.
You dream in colors
never found in North America.
You miss things you've never known:
the gray crowns of whistling thorn,
gazelles running in late afternoon.
You can forget what you do see,
all the meaningless words you hear.
You turn to soft dark places,
climb down your tree into night,
stars sparkling like crystal grapes,
the moist earth fragrant,
stretching out beneath your paws.
The run, the kill,
the struggle as you open up the warm belly.
Your heart splitting like a drum,
you almost taste the blood,
almost remember who you are.

Bison bison

In the distance the mud clouds
moved like sails
on a long line of wind.
And all the visions that spell
America young,
the visions that darkness tricks
out of any convenient corner
fell onto their backs,
a cargo against powerlessness.
All along the musculature of Oklahoma,
Kansas, Minnesota, skin of Texas,
arms of Colorado, old skeletons
told of men sweeping up, stepping from clouds,
changing the rhythm of hooves the same way
thunder clapped it in them.
One giant muscle working its way across grassland,
their black-brown humps fell one by one,
a few lingering in greasy light.
Now under stars that spike clean sky,
their clutches grow sweet with calves
and they come again. The air opens to gunshot,
taking the world back to dead valleys
and proven sinners, of feverish attempts
at true beginnings, new towns born from dust.
These men again break it all open,
showing us a land of odd memories,
phantoms of what we wish
to forget as history.
They come again,
draining the fields, holding back failure,
holding their own lost youth
in clean white hands.

The Succession of the Oak

A naked oak in a northern sky
kicks open your eyes,
black lightning bolts exploding in all weather.
Like a beast, it makes the heart beat more
as if reaching for you, for heaven.
Across empty prairie it engulfs the mind
with a perfume exotic as any plumeria or star fruit tree.
It stands alone, dark jewel of the air,
reaching out as if to call to you, to whisper in your ear,
not to tell you how the world ends up,
but to tell you not to worry so much,
that somewhere there is unity,
to tell you that beyond the bitter wind
and the old crows picking at bones,
below in the deep black compost marvel of earth,
all trees touch.

Wild Flowers

Cold shoots through the soles of our shoes,
last year's oak leaves tremble like blots of Japanese paper.
We drag ourselves inside our glum winter skins
out between barren thickets and sweetness of new mud,
the world so big, who could believe it?
Naked hackberry, hard red pebbles of sumac,
thin whistle of ice on the pond still as stone
like the album of sad things that covered our past months,
the awful stillness that filled our bones.
But here by this tree, this rock, and jumble of wind,
we find a map. Tiny trillium, trout lily, false rue anemone,
their voices belling out over the dull plank of earth,
directing us to where the road begins, new.
And we choose our route, cold and innocent
as the greedy beaks of young birds,
trusting the coming wings of distant summer,
trusting the world to help catch us when we fall.

Before This

Laval, France

Before the minutes
waved like the sea
a slow rolling of beats
to time the flowering plum tree,

before the winds from the river
astonished the grasses
and the hooves of goats,

before the gray slate roof,
layered like feathers
covered all the beams,

before voices walked these rooms,
the color of fire,
the deep water of a cello,
dark pink floribunda roses
grew out below the willow
stopping at the line of crops,

the silence of the earth
pulling birds to nests of sunflowers,
the blue lights of their wings
ribbons in the young islands of chestnut.

Before everything we speak of
sinks further away
into the dark shell of memory,
we stop to hold this one moment
before it leaves,
like those who study their child
with longing before she eventually
slips beyond
the small door of their lives.

Töölon Hospital

Helsinki, Finland

I am the stranger in the room
who has not been raised
on the long sad winds of the Baltic.
I am not caught like my roommates
in the tiny orbit of my body,
my neck broken in a car accident
or by a drunken boyfriend.
My broken leg just lies there,
lifted by pillows like a bride to an altar.
I am the stranger in the room,
yet grief and longing seem to surround me here,
calling out ancestors that I never knew.
They appear one by one,
reaching down from my skin,
remembering this soil, remembering home;
the three sisters left behind in the old farmhouse,
the sauna in the back by the potato field,
the snow that hung in the air,
quiet sentences against the cold,
against all that was lacking,
that hunger that made them leave.
How they never forgot their music
or the figures of parents or wives
paralyzed in the doorway
watching them go.
I am the stranger in the room,
yet here I am, together with
my grandparents and great-grandparents
listing the maps of our lives
in these two countries on our fingertips.
The hospital clock stands before us,
its sweeping arms
claiming the here and now,
but this is a different language we share
and I am just beginning to understand.

Grandfather

Juhani Järvenpää 1890–1977

Your eyes brushed me,
flints of copper
warmed from the sun.
Just as I felt their graze
they would flip, curved wings, back inside.
You held there
past mysteries that entered
you in the low dust of the iron mine,
in the young voice of your wife
who trembled like smoke into death.
It was your eyes that caught my words
lying unspoken, a silent wind
in my throat.

Your hands
smoothed themselves through a cabin,
your fingers shaped the trees
into forms hugging the earth in memory,
sinking roots into the dirt of this country.
I find you in the faint scent of cedar,
in the high wave of grass by a field.

The fleeting of your shy gaze,
your arm that wrapped me in its shawl,
left me soft like pats of butter
from your farm.
My English tongue never knew the words.
It still wants to build you houseboats,
glide you to the old country,
bathe you with smoking birch and wet leaves,
sweet lakes bringing cool fire music,
fish and a woodwind sun.

You found here a land of birch,
tombs of iron ore,
sacrificial pits and sharp cut cries
of logging camps twisting the color of sun.
Growing old you sat quietly
your body gently swaying the bent rocker
with a smile men have when the fighting has calmed.
Tapping your cane before me,
you pulled on my shoulder,
slowed the pace of my young legs
and spread on my lap your hand,
its map of years and soundless words
the loudest language you could give.

My Grandmothers in America

Hilja Kuitunen Laitinen
and
Elissa Mattila Järvenpää

When I take you out
of the picture box
and set your faces before me,
standing in front of houses,
sitting with babies,
you are still only dreams of people
repeating in my parents;
the way my mother sings
the full cycle of your song,
the way my father's dark head
holds a deep distant wound.
Only dreams of people,
your lives taken long ago
as though the boats that brought
you to this country one day found you
ready to leave the barren Minnesota land
happy to wave goodbye to sickness,
a husband's tyranny.
All your photographs,
empty and unscented blow at my life
even in the delicate stretching of children
burning their bubble in you
and then set beside you before the camera's eye.
Still only starched portraits speak:
a locket of hair on a tired forehead,
hands clasped in knots.
Like swans in weedy bogs,
your inky eyes wait for inevitable escape,
the only visible parts
of your bodies
left for me to guess at
swimming in your children.

Flying Geese

In memory of Esther Tuttle Behnke 1836–1928

The candy box spills over with quilt pieces,
scissors cutting into all of your lives;
the imperfect parts of your world
back into your hands as triangles and squares,
the battlefield of your life
now recreated into perfect geometry.
On those nights the babies cried and cried
you can now stitch the assurance of sleep,
each panel petals of a flower
smoothed and arranged by your fingers.
As you sit in your chair sewing together
blue and pink tongues of cotton,
listening to gossip, you remember how you came
to the Midwest on that covered wagon,
the softness of the moon on your forehead,
how the family settled into the town of Free Thinkers,
the rhythms of German and Lakota filling your head.
Now you hold the very outer skins of your family
and bring them together once more
by the pull of your aging hands,
the needle pricks of blood smiles you let fall.
Plum and apple, chestnut and sugar beet,
colors you stitch into patterns of flying geese,
the spread-wing panels stacked into long strips,
stacked like a ladder to the heavens
so that you may hear as you reach the top
the sound of their many wings taking flight.

For Those of Us Left Behind

With life and life's taking there is a darkness
that comes when all you want are stars
and all you see is that hole that is sky.
And dreams are how sunlight once felt
and time the longest bus ride across the prairie.
Loss is death on loan to seed your night's
emptiest telling, working the wound
until you cannot touch it anymore,
its immortal dust shaking you awake.
Somehow beyond the sleeplessness,
you hope to imagine again
your body past the halfness;
losing the long dark run
and finding music,
measuring memory and making it sound,
children bursting like tree buds trusting light,
the silence filled and dream of spring.

The Rubble Women

Berlin 1945

They stood for hours at a time
in their dresses and high heels,
bending and lifting pieces of rubble
as though delivering up their own bodies.
Their hands hard and bone red
passed on the weight
like a birth gone wrong—
boulders, cornerstones, broken eye sockets
of buildings carried down the long line
that threaded itself through
the gray-dust leavings of the city.
Scarves knotted around hair,
they scooped up waste
as children tugged at their skirts,
pressing fragments of brickwork
into their own flesh.
They stood at their task like exiles
as unsure of sunlight
as all the other women led away forever
from the packed railway cars,
unsure in the long hard line
of yesterday's truth.
They were left behind
like a string of dancers at solstice,
to start over,
kneeling like their ancestors did
long before in the fields,
facing an empty sky.

Somewhere Someone Is Drinking Brandy

Here under the bridge
that swings across
the frozen water
nothing is as it seems.
The blue smoke from the factories
rides up, each stream set in a row
slicing the air with activity
but looking as lifeless
as just-blown candles.

Sitting at the lip of the river
empty soup cans and wine bottles
emerge from the snow crust
like tips of early crocus buds.

You feel the bridge rumble on your back
as cars and buses
push through lights,
endless exhaust of evening.
The rolling of tires from above
floats down,
low waves breaking
on a cracked sea wall.
You hear a distant dolphin scream.

Every day the years
burn out of sight
but remain forever suspended
in the bird's nest,
tracks of the old man walking the dog,
pausing to stare at the opposite shore.

As you feel
the cold vapor once again
walk around inside you
with the thud of a German boot,
you look at the city,
at the lights strung like pieces
of colored velvet,
turn to strike a new match,
open a new can.

Down to the River

Down to the river,
where reeds are tall and blond
and water rushes over pebbles.
Where young boys canoe and hook fish,
answering the long call of summer's siren
pulsing across the hills,
past all women, past the dry throats of teachers,
past the tame minds of suburbia.

Down to the river,
to lay at its curving knee,
and watch accipiters circle and glide
over this river that flows past the prison,
past the warden's house where his wife has coffee parties
and the inmates come to fix her kitchen floor,
past the rutabaga fields where the prisoners
dig in the golden days of October,
the sun licking their shoulders like honey.

Down to the river where it splits through farms,
where listless children dig for treasure
looking for arrowheads,
finding beer cans, used condoms
and empty hunting cartridges,
the failed dreams of dark earth and sandstone.
Down to the river, to every river,
the Yukon and the river Neva,
to follow every instinct
of those who came before,
breaking off branches of the river birch,
climbing up for the tiniest leaves.
Taking off clothes,
water slipping across skin
as one more skin.

And sleep at the river's edge,
dream of Sarajevo, Chiapas, Los Angeles, Rwanda,
dream of lichen, cinnamon ferns, northern lights, fireflies.
Dream of the river,
how it takes pain
and slams it against the rocks,
its mystery shaking us.
Dream of the river,
how we dam it,
how we watch it go.

Polka

It careens through the room,
a battery of barking dogs,
a cocktail shaker of notes on the page.
Its inheritance of sounds
slams you with its broken dam,
reuniting your legs with the old streets
of Lublin, Schweinfurt, Kangasniemi.
The accordion wiggles and drops
broken pieces of verbs,
calling up the essence of the thing itself,
the unwinding of pain and dead fathers.
Slapping the skin,
it groups its rhythm
like small bubbles in the blood,
a heaving forth of new language,
that one more chance at being born.

III

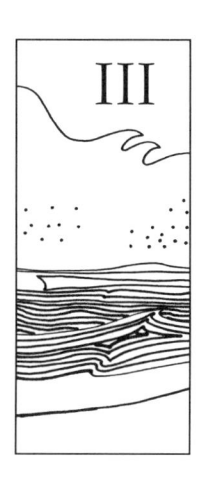

Aubade

I lie in bed the way animals
in winter sleep hidden in a ball,
my breathing loose and slow
around me.
You sit downstairs with your
coffee cup, a curl of steam,
silver in the dark,
waiting for morning
as one waits in the hot summer
for a storm to take the green sky.
And it comes slowly,
light peeling itself
from its pencil line of sun moving out
like a bead of butter.
You begin most days like this,
alone with your newspaper
and I in turn, follow you.
This is the unremarkable way
our days begin,
slow motions in a house
little different from the houses
next door, while the earth completely
changes around us.
But as you say good-bye,
handing off the morning to me
like a ball that fits perfectly
in my hand, columns of sunlight
begin to explode through the blinds
the way birds leave a tree all at once.
This is how my days begin,
standing at the window, stunned,
watching you leave it all behind
for me.

Bee Song

We lie in a maze of bee clover
that blooms like a speckled sky.
Plump, velvet bee bellies
hum around us as a thunder
rolls between us.
They suck the sugary white threads,
doze on bending stalks,
as we eye the infinite blue,
loose warm folded lips.
The lake's dark wet disk
shines below us
as we are locked together
inside this pink honey haze,
inside this field of grace notes,
inside the wind
of a hundred
wild
bee
sighs.

Wedding

Not even when I walked past the crowd
in lavender and lace,
Hawaiian flowers tipping at my brow,
did I think this was anything
beyond a ceremony we tricked out of the day,
a large photograph we composed for proof
of what we already knew.

Not even when we cut through
the sticky mass of layered cake,
its shimmering matte of pastels
warning us of vanity,
of the fullness of presence,
of the artfulness of solitude,
did we think something
lies there hidden like a laughing child.
I didn't notice,
in the ease of people shaking hands,
their bands of pink silks scooped by breeze,
what was different.

Whoever understands
what it means to choose a person
understands hedged bets,
the body beginning to break down and unfold,
to be somehow delivered up,
passed into this life
by the parade of all those hands,
the same kind that heal
a wounded raptor and let it go.

And we thought nothing changed that day
as we stood there
at the border of our world
slowly linked together
for the world to see,
totally ignoring the force of ritual
grabbing us on its long run.

Poem about Us from Samarkand
for Donald

On that day in July when
you knelt in thick Minnesota grass
pinching rose bushes,
I sat in a twin-engine plane
carving its hot body
over the lands of Tamerlane,
its cities shimmering blue silk
in the desert wind.
On that same day, with a sun so molten
it turned the streets into
ropes of smoking lava,
I sat in the shade of a plane-tree
staring at this face of earth
all flowers and clay.
I felt the past, long rivers
of the body remembering
as women started a fire for tea.
I saw old fingers stitch azure tiles
onto mausoleums lighting the way for the dead.
Walking narrow streets
I found fruit pits and gladiola stems,
the low song of men bent over chessboards and prayer,
the low song of women in constant movement.
And I wanted prayer and movement,
I wanted to endure myself
as the sands here endured all the bones;
I wanted to auction off all the young fears
that rock nights, making them ring empty
as a cracked bell.
And there in that street winding out
like unloosened hair, you entered
the pure event of my retreat.
Like rain falling from a sky dry as moon skin
I stopped walking and thought of you,
continents away, lying in our bed,
understanding the flickering of my youth.
I felt like someone woke me from a long dream,

the weight of my nights breaking like a slow wave.
As night opened itself on my shoulders,
the earth's face fringing me with its shawl,
I felt in need of nothing,
like the city, all stillness,
all new.

Uspenski Cathedral

Helsinki

for N.

As you came
to paintings of Christ
you kissed each one.
You told me of Cyprus,
your family hiding in the caves
when you were ten,
darkness madly strewn across all the hours,
relatives raped and murdered.
I sat in silence as you prayed
and like an ancient traveler
scoring over maps
stumbling onto a village
and a dozen more ways
to see a woman,
taste fruit, hear the dances of god,
I could see the candles
lit in every hand,
hear slow minor harmonies
slipping from tongues.
You smiled at me
as the sun drilled its afternoon eye
through the church glass,
its great wing of light
attending to your wounds.

Bathtub on Rue Tolosane

I slip my bones into water,
spine pressed to the slick flank of marble,
arms wing-like, fanning at the heat.
Through the open window
sounds of painters across the alley way,
shoes clopping on cobblestones below
and the clanging of bread pans from the boulangerie
fill the air with swear words and *gros pain*.
Sinking deeper, muscles untightening to what stillness is,
it is my turn to start the ritual, plunged into my own sea,
releasing all that fear that gathers on the skin.
Here in the bathtub where we plan to heal ourselves,
where prayer and blessing can come
to the flesh all child-like and wanting,
I sing loose and loud
I Ain't Got Nothing But the Blues,
ribbons of Ellington, passing around 17th century walls,
lifting an inner weight as I cross
from traveler's exhaustion to journey's end.
Stepping out, rinsed and ready for day,
the bathtub holds what I've left behind, like so many,
my unneeded dust and struggles for life to make sense,
and the water there,
still somehow shimmering.

The Accordion Repairman

Almost losing her to the night
you catch her fall
with hands that pilot over
all the buttons and fine-toothed keys.
With each draw you sense
burning at the window,
some stumble and spit
as you push out the lonely air
like old cigar smoke.
She bares the dark cave of her reeds,
her vest of silver flowers shining like spillage.
The moment you take her in your arms,
her voice navigates the room,
leaving archipelagoes of sound,
an outdoor restaurant with a dance floor
where you passed the small storm of your youth,
dancing beneath the lanterns,
weightless and immortal as the heavens.

Sudden Wealth

This white cliff of flour an impediment to sadness,
coastal cries of seagulls piercing through the sifter
and the many dozen eggs, remote sunset yolks
making you dizzy with that naked yellow
at the bottom of the bowl.
And the other puddle of clear albumen,
innocence before the whirling dervish prayer
of silver beaters spinning angel wings of frothy domes.
Your simple hands proofing desire
with each cupful of sugar,
music of vanilla and framboise,
tireless dream of the wooden spoon,
smoothing lumps, beating the unwanted.
Down to that greatest pleasure of uncontrolled need,
visitation of pure patience double-boiler warm—
chocolate—melting every syllable of night, of sex,
of handfuls of earth and roses.
They all come together before you
from the bowl of primordial ooze
to the rich disks of dark moons
lacquered and glossy as wet stones,
touched with the blood of raspberries.
All sadness long gone
as the fork finds the cake and
that passage to sudden wealth.

Past Time

We swarm the stadium
with the hum of many bees
around this childhood confection,
tearing shreds of cotton candy
and sipping beer from a ballpark paper cup,
infused with a feeling of time in perfect slo-mo.
We feed on the leisurely
chess-like rhythm of each inning
as the starter warms up nerves and tendons
into a delirious let go. Pop.
The ball is sucked past the batter.
We pray for the pitcher like a soul in purgatory,
just one shutout and his ascent is a done deal.
The collective sighs lull us,
the grand slams make us see stars in the velvet sky
lying beyond that pale skin dome.
It is not so much a tonic
for the nagging hiss of big city on-ramps
or the white noise of our personal defeats
as it is a neighborhood, transformed before us
with chalk bases and bucktoothed kids.
It is a step back into the vent of our past,
a look at the parallel life that follows us daily,
that younger self, small and skinned-kneed
who maybe never hit a split finger fast ball
or rounded the horn with lightning shoes,
but always knew how the body can work miracles
in the smallest most elegant ways.

La'a Kea Farm
Nahiku, Maui

Around the certainty of jungle,
uluhe and wild ginger reach out
under the tangle of half-light,
air a delicate wet
like parachute silk dropping on our skin.
Hibiscus open their mouths into our hands
the breath of something unnamed
under this sun that hangs close like ripe fruit.
The arms of the island hold the scattered bits of stars
close for us to see in the slim fever of night.
Each day we are drenched
by the breath of flowers
breaking in us
wave on wave 'ilima, 'awapuwi, lehua.
Our bodies lean away from sea,
open to the shimmering brushstrokes
of green, pale green and palm.
Blending with the rivers
we taste the soil and let it go,
give it up
like the heliconia shorn for market.
We become nameless,
without past or future,
perfect for the picking.

Orchidaceae

It lifts itself from the dark crumble of bark,
winching each blossom
out of pieces of sunlight, air, dust;
floating stories of the epiphyte
hooked onto the side of a great wet and hairy tree.
Beyond all sensibility, drops of glamour form,
delicate wings of petals open.
Fleshy green tongues of leaves,
long life muscles formed in space, drinking mist,
guide those in sticky flight
to the bulge of mouth,
lacquered bowl, frilled lung
that spills outward that surge of energy;
pollen in fat waxy masses, sweet buds of dreams.
Like shy birds looking down at you from the trees,
they illuminate the darkness, breathing,
whispering how one can make much out of thin air.

Vernal Equinox

Like the ginkgo wearing the weight
of all the years still supple green,
it goes on like this,
the red crack of tulips,
a sharp stigmata in the earth's brown body,

it goes on,
light swelling candelabras of sun,
a lemon-tangerine perfume
waking sleeping women
and fish caught in mud;

it goes on
the way of a man
staggering under high noon,
fantasy and pain
uttered in total agreement

and the new spring sky open
to all the burning eyes
that wait in trees
for their chance beyond midwifery
and wild hepatica.

It goes on,
our hunger under pure yellow,
swift to eclipse
the soft prayers of the forest
lying ready to be eaten,
all willing sacrifice, all echoing
into the cups of our hands.

Summer Comes

Tiny spiders balloon off my finger,
the invisible thread tethered
to some island in thin air,
to some speck like a word almost uttered,
to some tunnel leading out
to another world just the same,
where seeds germinate
under the warm press of earth
and swallowtails drink at the raspberry bush.
Where summer comes
and blooms over great sadness
and opens the shell of the cycle of living,
not asking for praise or sympathy,
not asking anything special
just plainly speaking its name.
Its hot voice seals
the dark scars of winter
and the wheel of my body turns,
spinning every surface
to face the flame.

Things We Think We Cannot See

1. Dandelions

Around the corolla of dandelions
the blue sky and my fist
wrapped fat at the stems.
The flowers bounce as I run,
my feet slowly making contact
with each neighbor's yard:
McLaughlin's, then Metz's, then Schluter's.
Until I reach the back door,
the dog jumping
and my mother sitting at the kitchen table
on the telephone
her hand mid-air in an emphatic point
coming down to meet
my small hands letting go;
to understand all that is given,
that complete moment of surrender.

2. Gooseberries

Gooseberry bushes snarl up the backlot,
their green drops, sour pleasure
on young tongues.
We two girls, best friends, shudder among the wasps,
disbelieving our smallness.
We are pirates, our white blouses sailmasts
to our invisible suburban enemies.
Catbirds are the first mates
and balance seems to be everything,
what keeps us from tipping into
the cold waters of our mothers' voices
calling, calling us inside,
to leave our first mates in the honeysuckle
guarding the pearls and gold
we worked so hard to find.
Crowns of hawkweed and piles of gooseberries
left to whither under the crabapple tree,
the small green moons half-glittering
onto a world that keeps changing before us.

3. Wolves

Today my father saw wolves on the French River.
He looked up from his notes and there they were,
three, very close to where he was working.
Slowly walking the linoleum hallways of the nursing home
there are great green hills he doesn't know if he can climb.
Still he takes daily walks of many miles,
the Parkinson's traveling his body, working against the mind.
Syllables of words bubble to the surface and vanish
downstream, never mute, just out of reach,
unanswerable to all the loss.
Wandering into other patient's rooms;
hawks and fields, everything going on under blue sky.
He lies down to nap near mellow river sound,
leaves shaking off a scarlet and pear-color dance.
The old hunger on the rivers,
the brush with which he has been left
to paint whatever he needs.
At each vista the moon hangs just for him.

4. Garden

We are changed
by the ground that swells here
in smoky greens,
the sunlight fat and bruised
through the leaf prints,
touching our hands, touching
these cool nights
that pour themselves black
and enormous with stars
just balanced.
We have grown tangled
in the strawberries,
tender leaves of velvet lettuce,
we've been evolving in the dirt
in the way nasturtiums
start with the round pearl seed
and end with the flower stretched open,

giving up its darkness.
Here we are neither mythical
nor scientific, but a moment
standing still,
like this garden
speechless before dawn.

5. Red Oak

Her roots cracked and swirling mid-air
still hold the ground. Garter snakes slowly
thrum under flints of burnt umber leaves
lining the cool forest floor.
An anchored ship waiting patient waters,
she rests on her back, sure of her place,
arms stretched out,
catching wind in her fingers.
We climb inside
the dark box of her trunk,
a brimming potlatch bowl.
Standing on her damp walls,
the earth seems full of pulsing,
of thickening twig,
the storm of leaves that move
the boundaries in the ground
with their dull red wheels.
We feel we are in a cradle
rocked by a mysterious prayer
that comes to a day
and leaves just as quickly,
like the distant beating of aspen,
water coming to take up your body
in the woods,
coming to set you sail.

Divining the Landscape

Chin deep
in coneflowers and wild asters
we walk behind the monarchs,
their many wings enfolding space.
As we stand still
holding open our hands
they come to try to drink our sugar,
pulse their flaming dust
and rise to seek the edge
of still another place to get the rich food,
another bed to catch the body,
another point from which to spy
the morning tremble.
Divining at the end
of all the difficult miles,
the lonely nights over water,
there is always
another landscape to hold fast,
there is always
one more.

After the Concert

"Real singing is a different movement of air.
Air moving around nothing. A breathing in a god. A wind."
                                                    RILKE

You become more careful
walking through a room
where music is playing.
Don't make the record skip,
the earth is tipping already.
Step slowly,
like wading through an island
of white campion,
the sky misted with a low wind
and sea birds.
The world is now understood.
Beyond the sound that opens
the body into weightlessness—
a shadow lingers
in the region of the heart
that can't retreat—
a burning reflection of a storm
bursting,
leaving behind silent flowers
heavy with hunger.

Diane Jarvenpa was born in St. Paul, Minnesota in 1959. She has been published in various poetry journals and anthologies. She is a singer/songwriter who records under the name Diane Jarvi. This collection is her first book of poetry. She currently lives with her husband in Minneapolis.